FLYING FREE

FLYING FREE

America's First Black Aviators

by Philip S. Hart
foreword by Reeve Lindbergh

 Lerner Publications Company ▪ Minneapolis, Minnesota

To James Herman Banning, his sister, Virginia, and his nieces, Murlee and Pearl, who, all in their own unique ways, helped me start my journey

Library of Congress Cataloging-in-Publication Data

Hart, Philip S.
    Flying free : America's first black aviators / by Philip S. Hart ;
with a foreword by Reeve Lindbergh.
        p.   cm.
    Includes index.
    Summary: Surveys the history of black aviators, from the early
black aviation communities in Los Angeles and Chicago in the 1920s
through World War II to modern times.
    ISBN 0-8225-1598-9
    1. Afro-American air pilots—Juvenile literature. [1. Afro-
American air pilots.] I. Title.
TL521.H37   1992
629.13'089'96073—dc20   91-21433
                                                                CIP
                                                                AC

Manufactured in the United States of America

    2   3   4   5   6   7   8   98   97   96   95   94   93

Contents

FOREWORD
by Reeve Lindbergh

*L*ike Philip Hart, author of the book you are about to read, I grew up in a family that was involved in American aviation from its earliest days. My father, Charles Lindbergh, was the first person to fly solo nonstop across the Atlantic Ocean. Maybe that's why I have always held the belief that every child was born to fly. Of course, we don't all grow up to become pilots. But I am convinced that each and every young person has that same spark of courage and determination that sent the early pilots, like my father and Philip Hart's great uncle, James Herman Banning, into the skies.

Nobody ever said flying was easy. It takes time to find your wings. It also takes patience, endurance, and sometimes a little help from a friend. My father might never have made it across the Atlantic Ocean without the enthusiastic support of the St. Louis businessmen who put up the money to build his airplane. Bessie Coleman certainly would have had a much harder time learning to fly without the assistance of Robert S. Abbott. Herman Banning had the best help of all: the advice and encouragement of his father and the strength of his family behind him.

Whatever it took, they did it. They rose up like eagles, these early aviators of the 1920s and 1930s. They had to contend with bad weather, faulty and experimental airplanes, and the lack of sophisticated flight instruments. There were no modern maps or flight plans or radio communications with airport control towers—often there were no airports! A farmer's field somewhere at the edge of town was a common place to land a plane at the end of the day. And these early aviators were happy to arrive there safely.

They were adventurers, risk-takers, pioneers, daredevils, "flying fools"—any name you want to call them. The one thing they had in common was the burning desire to fly an airplane.

The early black pilots described in this book had another battle to fight, apart from bad weather and poor machinery. To reach the freedom of the air, they had to overcome racial prejudice on the ground. This book tells the story of how the first black aviators did just that. In their struggle, they showed a bravery and a strength of character that surpass any aviation feat I can imagine.

It took courage for my father to fly solo from New York to Paris in 1927. But Bessie Coleman needed just as much courage to earn her pilot's license in 1922, at a time when women—especially black women—weren't supposed to fly airplanes at all.

This book is more than an exciting record of a part of aviation history that has not been widely available to us until now. It is also a remarkable salute to the pioneer black aviators— people who found their wings and learned to fly free.

THE EARLY YEARS

Two early black aviators from Chicago

> The great bird will first take flight from the back of the great
> swan, filling the universe with amazement and all writings
> with its fame and bringing eternal glory to the nest where it
> was born.

*T*hese words were written by inventor, scientist, painter, and writer
Leonardo da Vinci more than four centuries ago. Da Vinci was
fascinated by the flight of birds, and he even envisioned a machine
that would give humans the freedom of flight. Da Vinci was clearly
a man ahead of his time.

Black aviators from the 1920s and 1930s were also ahead of their
time. These aviators were special people who rarely received the fame
or glory they deserved. This book tells the story of America's first
black aviators—people who took to the sky—flyers in search of a dream.

Leonardo da Vinci's vision began to take shape on a bright spring day in 1783. On that day, the Montgolfier brothers' hot-air balloon rose 6,000 feet (1,828 meters) above Annonay, France. These early balloonists led the way for Sir George Cayley of England, who, in 1853, successfully tested a glider—an engineless aircraft—of his own design.

Experiments to produce heavier-than-air flying machines continued throughout the 1800s. But powered flight didn't become possible until the introduction of the automobile engine in the late 19th century.

On a cold December morning in 1903, at Kitty Hawk, North Carolina, two young bicycle mechanics named Wilbur and Orville Wright made the first powered airplane flight. And history began a new chapter.

*The Wright brothers test their **Flyer** at Kitty Hawk.*

Airplanes took many shapes and forms in the early days. Some aircraft had wings that flapped like those of a bird. Other planes were nothing more than giant kites. Since the early pioneers built by guesswork, without much knowledge of the principles of flight, it's a wonder that so many of their airplanes flew at all. And it's even more of a wonder that many of the pilots walked away unharmed from the planes that crashed.

At first, private citizens built their own flying machines. When World War I broke out in Europe in 1914, many governments began to produce airplanes for military use.

The United States entered the war in 1917. At the time, the U.S. military was racially segregated—black and white soldiers served in separate units. And black soldiers were barred from many military jobs —including pilot. Because of this racial discrimination, a black American named Eugene Bullard chose to serve with the French air service during World War I. He was awarded the croix de guerre, the highest honor given by the French military, for his achievements in aviation combat.

As aviation became more widespread, more and more people, including blacks, became involved. By the end of World War I, black Americans wanted to fly, and they were willing to do just about anything for that opportunity. Against them, of course, was a large part of American society—a society noted for segregation and bias.

Many white people believed that blacks lacked the skills to be pilots. Blacks were not accepted in American flight schools. Few experienced pilots would teach blacks to fly on a private basis, and U.S. military flight training was closed off to them. Black people had to go to extraordinary lengths to obtain their pilot's licenses.

Richard Wright speaks of this discrimination in his 1940 novel, *Native Son*. Wright tells the story of two black youths who watch in frustration as a white pilot performs skywriting tricks high above them: "I could fly a plane if I had a chance," the first youth says.

"If you wasn't black and if you had some money and if they'd let you in that aviation school, you could fly that plane," his friend replies.

Pioneer aviators Eugene Bullard (above) and Charles Lindbergh (left)

The most common early airplanes were made of steel and wood, and they had fabric-covered wings. As airplanes became lighter, stronger, and faster, aviation became more popular. The 1920s and 1930s were known as the "golden age of aviation." This was a romantic time when flying was still somewhat new, and pilots were considered heroes.

Black aviators worked hard to earn their wings in the 1920s and 1930s. But their accomplishments were overshadowed by the transatlantic flights of Charles Lindbergh and Amelia Earhart, the round-the-world flights of Wiley Post, and the feats of other white flyers.

Still, many white pilots of the day recognized the skills of the black aviators and knew that most of the black pilots could not afford top-quality airplanes. Early black aviator Marie Dickerson Coker remembered: "The old planes were made out of wood, nylon—I don't even think it was nylon. And we just took chances flying around."

Coker recalled the thrill of flying in the 1920s and 1930s and remembered how exciting it was to see black people fly airplanes. The public, too, was intrigued by the sight of black pilots. The second all-black air show, held in December 1931 in Los Angeles, California, attracted more than 15,000 spectators.

In the days before airports, control towers, and radar, aviators landed in fields and farmland.

Beginning in the early 1930s, black pilots in Los Angeles put on air circuses and tried to promote aviation in the black community.

In addition to putting on air shows, early black aviators in Los Angeles and Chicago organized flight schools. Los Angeles was the site of the first all-black aero club, which formed in 1929. The Chicago flyers formed a club in the early 1930s.

But the story of black aviation is more than a list of the first black pilots to fly across the country or the first black parachutists to jump out of an airplane. The work of the early black aviators can also be seen as an attempt by blacks to gain equality in American society. For many blacks felt that if they could achieve equality in the sky, then equality on the ground would not be far behind.

During the early years of aviation, a number of black Americans became pilots. There are four who stand out: Bessie Coleman, William J. Powell, James Herman Banning, and Hubert Julian.

BESSIE COLEMAN

The Inspiration

During the golden age of the 1920s and 1930s, unlike any other time in the history of aviation, female pilots were almost as famous as the men. Among black pilots the situation was no different.

Black women were leaders in the first all-black aero clubs in both Los Angeles and Chicago. In fact, the primary inspiration in the formation of these clubs was a female pilot named Bessie Coleman. Indeed, Coleman was an inspiration to all black pilots during the golden age of aviation.

Bessie Coleman was born on January 26, 1893, in Atlanta, Texas. Bessie's mother was black. Her father was one-quarter black and three-quarters American Indian. Bessie was only seven years old when her father left Texas and returned to Oklahoma, or "Indian Territory" as the state was then known. Bessie's mother, Susan, refused to follow her husband. She stayed in Texas to raise her son and four daughters.

Bessie was one of those children who seem to be born with a drive to better themselves. Bessie loved to read. When she was very young, Bessie knew that she wanted to attend college.

After finishing high school, Bessie enrolled in Langston Industrial College, an all-black school in Oklahoma. Langston was founded on the idea put forth by Booker T. Washington that former slaves needed job training in order to succeed.

Running short of money, Coleman was able to attend college for only one semester. In 1912 she left Oklahoma and went to live with her brother in Chicago. There, Coleman trained to be a beautician. After completing her schooling, she went to work as a manicurist at the White Sox Barber Shop.

During World War I, Coleman saw newsreel films of military airplanes and began thinking about learning to fly. By the end of the war, in 1918, she had made up her mind to become a pilot. But because Coleman was black and because she was a woman, no flight school in Chicago would accept her.

Among white aviators, though, women had been quick to join men in the air. In 1784, Elisabeth Thible of Lyons, France, became the first woman to travel aloft in a hot-air balloon. In 1909, another French woman, Raymonde de Laroche, became the first licensed female pilot.

Coleman's early idol was Harriet Quimby. On August 2, 1911, Quimby earned her license from the Fédération Aéronautique Internationale, or International Aviation Federation, based in France. She became the first American woman with a pilot's license. Unfortunately, Quimby was killed less than a year later when her plane crashed into Boston's Dorchester Bay as she prepared for an air show.

Despite the accomplishments of Quimby and other female flyers, most people saw aviation as a man's game—and a white man's game at that. However, Coleman refused to become discouraged. She took a second job, at a chili parlor in Chicago, to save money for flying lessons. Coleman was sure she would eventually locate a flight school that would take her as a student.

Despite voices of discouragement, a number of women, such as record-setters Amelia Earhart (top) and Harriet Quimby (bottom), became pilots in the early days.

In 1920, Coleman was fortunate to meet one of the wealthiest black men in Chicago, Robert S. Abbott. Abbott published the *Chicago Defender*, a successful black newspaper, and he liked the idea of a black woman becoming an airplane pilot.

Abbott helped Coleman contact an aviation school in France, and he advised her to learn some French. Abbott knew that the French were more open-minded than Americans in matters of racial and sexual equality.

With Abbott's help, and with the savings from her two jobs, Coleman went to Europe in 1921. There, she trained with some of the best pilots in France. She returned to Chicago for a few months before traveling to Europe once more.

On this trip, in 1922, Coleman took flying lessons from the chief pilot for Germany's Fokker aircraft company. By the time she returned from her second trip abroad, Coleman had earned her license from the Fédération Aéronautique Internationale. She became the world's first black woman with a pilot's license.

Coleman thus joined a handful of American aviators who took flying seriously when most people considered it only a curiosity. In fact, the United States Department of Commerce did not begin licensing pilots in the U.S. until 1926.

Coleman's primary aim when she returned from France was to start a flight school for black men and women. As her fame slowly grew, Coleman dreamed of the day when her school would open.

But Coleman needed money to open a school. To raise funds, she proposed giving exhibitions, or air shows. Although her family was against the idea, Coleman gave her first exhibition at Chicago's Checkerboard Field in 1922. Robert S. Abbott, proud as a father, was there beaming with excitement. Photographers and writers from Abbott's newspaper attended in full force.

The show went well, and Coleman was encouraged when several young black men expressed an interest in learning to fly. Coleman told them that unless some blacks with vision provided the funds, the flight school would have to wait until she raised the money herself.

Coleman was featured in the *Defender* that week. The novelty of a female airplane pilot made an exciting story. The newspaper coverage also helped Coleman reach the black population with a message about opportunities in the new field of aviation.

After giving other exhibitions in the Chicago area, Coleman decided to head south. With Houston, Texas, as her base of operations, Coleman began to barnstorm, or exhibit, in new territory.

Barnstormers have often been called airborne gypsies. These pilots traveled across the country, performing at fairs and carnivals. If they found no carnival for their exhibitions, they would attract crowds on their own with aerobatic stunts, wing-walking, and parachute jumps. They would pass the hat for donations or talk the local people (those who were brave enough) into paying for an airplane ride. Moving on to new locations, they would land in farmers' fields and sleep in barns— thus the term "barnstorming."

Barnstorming was not a safe way to make a living. There were broken wing struts and faulty engines, ripped fabric and collapsed landing gear. There were crowds of people, most who knew nothing about flying, who would spill onto the landing field, often in the path of the oncoming airplane. Many spectators seemed to be more attracted by the possibility of a crash than by the opportunity to see skillful flying.

As a barnstormer and stunt pilot, Coleman began crisscrossing the country, encouraging other black people to take up aviation. Between flights, she lectured on aviation in churches and movie theaters.

In 1924, Coleman was barnstorming in California and doing aerial advertising for the Firestone Tire & Rubber Company when she had her first plane crash. She was forced to take a year off to recover from facial cuts, broken ribs, and a fractured left leg.

During this time, Coleman spoke of starting an all-black flight school in Los Angeles. The city was becoming a center of aviation activity. But Coleman still needed to raise a lot more money before she could put her dream into action. So, when her injuries healed in early 1925, Coleman took off across the country once more.

Adding to the dangers of flight, barnstormers performed daredevil stunts like wing-walking.

She traveled to Florida and performed around the state throughout the next year. In April 1926, the Jacksonville Negro Welfare League asked Coleman to give an exhibition. The proceeds from the air show, when added to the funds Coleman had already raised, would give her enough money start a flight school in Los Angeles. She was excited and began to prepare for the show almost immediately.

Rehearsing on the evening of April 30, 1926, flying at 110 miles (177 kilometers) per hour at an altitude of 3,500 feet (1,067 m), Coleman put her plane into a nosedive. But instead of righting itself at the end of the dive, the plane continued downward and flipped upside down.

Coleman was not wearing a parachute or a seat belt. She was thrown out of the airplane, 2,000 feet (610 m) above the ground. Life ended for Bessie Coleman, at age 33, on a warm spring evening in Jacksonville.

She had come close to realizing her dream of starting an all-black flight school. But instead, Coleman met a fate similar to that of her idol, Harriet Quimby. It was a fate that hundreds of daring men and women met during those adventurous early days of aviation.

Coleman's life was brief, but it had been full. And she had succeeded in inspiring members of her race to carry on in the field of aviation. Coleman's family brought her body back to Chicago for burial. For many years after Bessie Coleman's death, black pilots would fly over her grave site each Memorial Day and drop a floral wreath in her honor. She is remembered in this anonymous verse:

> High up into the azure skies,
>> Amid the April clouds,
> The man-invented plane-bird flies,
>> Above the watching crowds.
> With steady hand the pilot guides,
>> And higher up it goes.
> Upon the milky way it glides,
>> And earth a greeting throws.
> A sudden nosedive in the air,
>> A guiding hand astray,
> And fate has worked its wicked snare,
>> On April's last spring day.
> Through space a pilot falls to earth,
>> And in the field lies dead.
> Around are stilled the shouts of mirth,
>> While silent tears are shed.

Bessie Coleman's influence was not forgotten. With her spirit in mind, a small group of aviation enthusiasts formed the first all-black flying association, the Bessie Coleman Aero Club, in Los Angeles in 1929.

Los Angeles was the perfect spot for such an aviation breakthrough. The city was the center of the nation's growing aviation industry. And between 1910 and 1920, the black population in Los Angeles had greatly increased. Many blacks came to the city during World War I, taking jobs in factories that produced airplanes and military equipment.

Bessie Coleman, shown here in her flight suit, is buried in Lincoln Cemetery in Chicago.

By 1920, the Central Avenue community of Los Angeles had a black YMCA, a black YWCA, a black hospital, and a branch of the National Negro Business League. Five black newspapers competed for readers. The most well known was the *California Eagle*. There were a dozen black social clubs and two dozen large black churches. Los Angeles attracted many of the best educated and most prominent black people in the United States.

One important member of the Los Angeles black community was a young businessman from Chicago named William J. Powell. Powell had a keen interest in aviation, and he had followed Bessie Coleman's career closely. Powell was one of the key organizers of the Bessie Coleman Aero Club and, like Coleman, he was a visionary.

WILLIAM J. POWELL

The Visionary

When World War I ended, the production of military airplanes slowed down. Many people who had worked in the aviation industry around Los Angeles found themselves unemployed.

But enthusiasm for aviation did not die down. Prior to 1919, most pilots built their own airplanes in barns, garages, or backyards. After World War I, these same people found that war-surplus aircraft cost less than home-built planes. In Los Angeles, there were a lot of surplus military airplanes and many people eager to fly them.

Pilots made a living, and kept aviation alive, by providing thrills and giving rides to the public. By carrying passengers, these pilots helped give rise to the airline industry that would emerge a decade later.

The movie industry was also booming in Los Angeles. Pilots provided a constant source of material for the early moviemakers, and black pilots were no exception.

"Race movies," films made especially for black audiences, were popular in the 1920s. One such film, *The Flying Ace*, was billed as "the greatest airplane mystery thriller ever made." Produced in 1926, the movie featured an all-black cast and was a classic tale of good versus evil. Both the good guy and the bad guy were pilots. Movies like *The Flying Ace* got a lot of black people interested in aviation. But few people took aviation more seriously than William Powell.

William J. Powell was born in Henderson, Kentucky, in 1897 and moved with his family to Chicago when he was eight years old. When William was 16, he graduated from Chicago's Wendell Phillips High School and applied to the engineering school at the University of Illinois at Champaign.

Edna Gayle, Powell's sister, recalled that the university accepted William without difficulty. But the dean of the engineering school told William that in order to succeed, he would have to work harder than the white students.

Powell stayed in school for several years. In 1917, when the United States entered World War I, Powell enlisted in officer training school in Chillicothe, Ohio, in a segregated unit. He left officer's school as a first lieutenant and was sent to fight in Europe. On the last day of his tour of duty, the black troops in Powell's unit were ordered to the front lines, and Powell was gassed by the enemy.

Powell came back to the United States to recover from the poison gas and, when he had returned to better health, he opened an automobile service station in Chicago. Eventually, Powell opened four service stations and a big garage.

In 1926, Powell traveled to Paris, France, for an American Legion convention. There, at Le Bourget Airfield, Powell took his first exhilarating ride in an airplane.

He returned to Chicago very excited about aviation and tried to locate a flight school that would accept him. But, just like Bessie Coleman, he could not find a school that would take a black student. After much difficulty, Powell was accepted at a flight school in

Los Angeles. The school's owners said they didn't care if Powell was purple—as long as he had $1,000 for tuition.

Powell had never fully recovered from his wartime gassing. Over the years his health suffered, and a doctor suggested to Powell that a dry climate, like Arizona or California, would help him. Powell decided to sell his businesses in Chicago and move to Los Angeles—where he could regain his health and learn to fly.

Powell's family thought he should have been content with his business success in Chicago. But he was not. He had been bitten by the aviation bug.

Los Angeles, with its sizeable black community, was ripe for businesspeople like William Powell. After learning to fly himself, Powell began to dream of organizing an all-black flight school in honor of Bessie Coleman.

William Powell clearly saw that flying was a wave of the future. He realized that aviation was a new technology with the potential to change society—both in the way people traveled and the way goods could be shipped. In addition, as a war veteran, Powell understood the importance of airplanes in military combat. Powell was anxious for blacks to enter this new field on the ground floor—to become pilots, mechanics, flight school owners, and airplane designers.

In 1929, the Bessie Coleman Aero Club opened in Los Angeles in a storefront on West Jefferson Boulevard. Powell's long-term vision for the club was quite ambitious. He and three other businessmen hoped to form more than 100 black aero clubs in different cities around the United States.

Powell and other black aviators saw the airplane not only as a method of transportation but also as a force for social change in the United States. They felt that if blacks could show they were capable pilots, segregation and discrimination against the black population would decrease. Powell expected that every black achievement in the air would bring improvements in race relations on the ground.

Powell put forth his ideas in a 1934 book, *Black Wings*, and a 1935

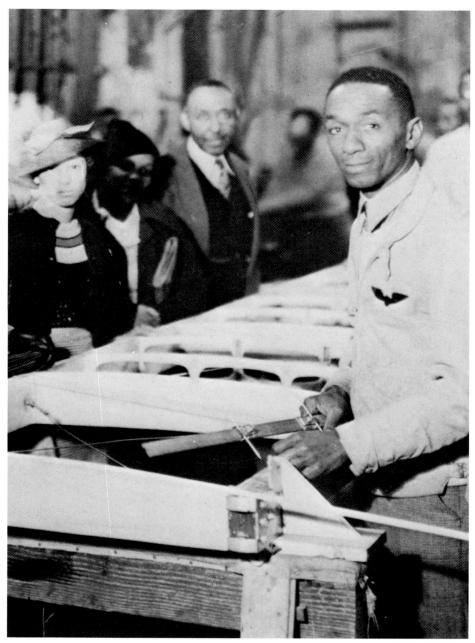

Powell at the Bessie Coleman Aero Club workshop, Los Angeles

Hoping to encourage the next generation of black aviators, Powell hoists a young boy into an airplane cockpit.

film, *Unemployment, the Negro, and Aviation.* Powell also published a newsletter called the *Craftsmen Aero News,* aimed at promoting aviation in the black community.

Marie Coker was among the first group of students at the Bessie Coleman Aero Club. She learned to fly in a biplane—an airplane with two sets of wings—capable of traveling at about 80 miles (130 km) per hour.

No matter what race a pilot was, he or she could always find an audience. The first all-black air show sponsored by the Bessie Coleman Aero Club took place in September 1931. The show attracted so much attention that Los Angeles city officials asked the club to put on a second exhibition as a benefit for the city's unemployment fund.

The second all-black air show was held on December 6, 1931, at Eastside Airport in Los Angeles. The show featured the "Black Eagle," Hubert Fauntleroy Julian, a well-known aviator from New York City, as well as big band music by the Frank Sebastian Orchestra from the Cotton Club in Harlem, New York.

The atmosphere was electric. While pilots performed stunts in the air, motorcycle daredevils jumped through hoops and performed other tricks on the ground. At the same time, the big band was playing up-tempo music in the stands. Marie Coker remembered the excitement:

> There were only five [black] people flying out here in California, and when Julian came out that made six. So there were Five Blackbirds and one parachute jumper....I would be the last one to go up. And everybody came to see this girl fly. I did my figure eights. I did my spiral....We were called the Five Blackbirds because that is the first time in history that five black people were in the air at one time.

Black and white pilots alike were determined to move aviation beyond air circuses and barnstorming. Long-distance endurance flights would show the true value of airplanes as a means of cross-country transportation. Black flyers such as William Powell, Hubert Julian, and an aviator named James Herman Banning longed to be the first of their race to fly coast to coast.

In *Black Wings*, Powell wrote that an endurance flight was a necessity to prove that blacks were capable aviators. But Powell's true vision for aviation relied on the next generation. His sister Edna explained:

> It wasn't the flying so much that he was interested in. It was trying to interest our young black boys in aviation, because he realized that's the future. And if our boys didn't get into it right away, they'd be left out.

JAMES HERMAN BANNING

The Adventurer

James Herman Banning was born in Canton, Oklahoma, on November 5, 1900. At the time, Oklahoma was known as "Indian Territory." Throughout the 19th century, Oklahoma was the dumping ground for Indian tribes that had been pushed off their land by white settlers and their increasing desire for territory.

After the Civil War, many black freedmen also moved to Oklahoma to homestead, or settle, the land. One was Riley W. Banning, who, with his wife Cora, arrived in central Oklahoma in the 1880s. After having four children—Archibald, Roy, Virginia, and James Herman—Riley and Cora Banning set their sights on securing their own land. Under the government Homestead Act, Riley Banning took ownership of 160 acres (73 hectares) of land in central Oklahoma near Kingfisher on December 31, 1903.

Riley and Cora constructed a small frame school building on their land, with room for 20 to 30 children. The class consisted of the Banning children and other black and Indian children from the area.

By 1907, James Herman had started school on the family homestead. He was a soft-spoken child with an interest in both reading and mathematics. He enjoyed tinkering with farm machinery, even at an early age. Among the materials used in school were books on automobile mechanics. Young James Herman loved leafing through these books, looking at the pictures.

In the fall of 1916, James Herman traveled east from Kingfisher to attend Faver High School in Guthrie, Oklahoma. There, he continued to study mathematics, and his ability to repair automobiles and farm equipment improved. As the spring of 1917 approached, and James Herman was nearing the end of the 11th grade, the United States entered World War I. The U.S. Army began to build up its aviation division.

James Herman Banning (left rear) and his family in Canton, Oklahoma, 1917

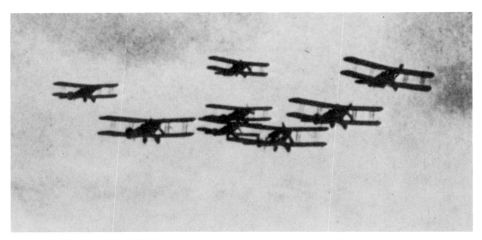

Films of World War I combat planes inspired Banning to learn to fly.

By then, Germany, France, Russia, Great Britain, and Belgium, which had entered the war several years earlier, were far ahead of the Americans in military aviation. Every chance he had, Banning ran to the movie theater, not for the feature film, but for the newsreels. James Herman relished watching newsreel footage and seeing the German, French, and British aircraft duel in the European sky.

Soon Banning began to seek out more information on aviation. He read about aviation pioneers like the Wright brothers and Glenn Curtiss, who had designed and built the popular Curtiss JN-4D, or "Jenny." Banning became obsessed with flying machines.

By the time he entered his final year of high school in the fall of 1918, James Herman had become a skilled automobile mechanic. In addition, his grades suggested that he had a good chance for success in college. He continued to learn all he could about aviation, but most of his time was spent tinkering with automobiles and farm equipment.

Banning finished high school in the spring of 1918. Because of his mechanical abilities and his good marks in mathematics, he hoped to study engineering at college. But Banning's sister and two brothers had left the homestead, and much of the work around the farm fell on his shoulders. Instead of going directly to college, he spent a year on the farm and earned money doing odd jobs as a mechanic.

By the spring of 1919, Banning had saved nearly $1,000 and was ready to continue with his schooling. He considered nearby Langston College and Tuskegee Institute in Alabama, both all-black colleges with good engineering programs. He also applied to Iowa State College in Ames—although he did not think he would be admitted.

Iowa State had a strong engineering program. In addition, Iowa was a fertile ground for aviation activities. As early as 1845, a hot-air balloon was sent up without passengers at Burlington, Iowa. Beginning in 1910, barnstormers flew aircraft at county fairgrounds and other suitable fields around the state. By 1919, Iowa was a hotbed of aviation activity.

Banning was pleased to learn that Iowa State had accepted his application. Following his father's advice and encouragement, he decided to attend the college. Riley and Cora Banning rented their homestead to another family and moved with their son to Iowa.

Ames was a pleasant town with an open attitude toward black Americans. With relatively little difficulty, the Bannings found a home on West Second Street. Young Banning began his freshman year at Iowa State as one of only a handful of black students.

While attending school, Banning continued to work as a mechanic. He set up shop in his parents' garage, and his skills became well known in the Ames area. In the meantime, Riley Banning purchased a 1915 Iver-Johnson motorcycle for his son. James Herman Banning soon became a regular sight riding around Ames on his motorcycle.

In the spring of 1920, Banning took his first airplane ride. Stanley M. Doyle, a former World War I combat pilot, had come to Ames to fly in an air circus. After paying five dollars, Banning hopped into Doyle's Canuck biplane, and the two men took off for the blue skies. The 45-minute flight over the Iowa countryside was a thrill for Banning.

Doyle landed the Canuck safely, and Banning's parents ran to their son's side, grateful that he had returned to the ground unharmed. Banning was full of questions about aviation, but Doyle was unable to

answer them. A long line of people, encouraged by Banning's display
of bravery, eagerly waited for Doyle to take them flying.

Banning soon encountered Stanley Doyle again, at a football game in
Des Moines between Iowa State and Doyle's school, Drake University.
At halftime, Doyle dove his Canuck into Drake Stadium and dropped a
papier-mache bulldog, Drake's mascot, fitted with a parachute of blue
and white, the school colors. This stunt excited the spectators, including
Banning. As he sped back to Ames on his motorcycle, Banning couldn't
remove the vision of the airplane from his head. All he talked about
during the next few days was Doyle's bravery and daring.

As his auto repair business grew, Banning found that more and more
of his time was devoted to making money as a mechanic. He was spending so much time at his garage that his grades in school began to suffer.
After consulting with his parents, Banning decided to leave college
and devote his full attention to automobile repair. He formally opened
J. H. Banning's Auto Repair on West Second Street in Ames in 1921.

The repair shop began to prosper and soon required more space.
Banning located a suitable garage and moved his business to Fourth
Street. Meanwhile, several young kids in Ames began showing an interest in aviation. Before long, the repair shop was filled with young white
boys who wanted Banning to tell them more about airplanes.

Banning's knowledge about aviation was mainly secondhand. He read
everything he could find on this new and exciting field, and he attended
nearly every air circus in the Ames area. The fact that Banning couldn't
fly himself and had flown with other pilots only a few times did not
discourage his young admirers.

As 1923 drew to a close, Banning became more convinced that he
would learn to fly. He wasn't sure how difficult this task would be,
however. Banning had never seen a black pilot, but he had come across
the names of Eugene Bullard and Bessie Coleman. He read in the
Chicago Defender that Bullard had flown for the French in World War I
and that Coleman had learned to fly in France. Bullard and Coleman
seemed like distant visions to Banning. Surely, he did not have to go

all the way to France to learn to fly! But if he had to, then he would do just that.

By the winter of 1924, Banning was losing interest in motorcycles and automobiles. After spending considerable time trying—unsuccessfully—to locate a flight school that would accept him as a student, Banning persuaded a World War I veteran, Lieutenant Raymond C. Fisher, to teach him to fly.

That winter, in between blizzards, Banning would travel the snowy roads from Ames to Des Moines to train in an old Hummingbird airplane. In a 1932 interview with the *Pittsburgh Courier*, Banning recalled:

> There I would shiver and shake through a half hour dual instruction. Cold weather gave my natural shivering instincts quite an outlet. I need not mention the added shiverability provided by the shaking, trembling, dilapidated old plane in which we trained.

Banning at the controls of his first airplane, **Miss Ames**

Banning had saved enough money from his auto repair business to purchase his own Iowa-built Hummingbird biplane. He named it *Miss Ames*. When the U.S. Department of Commerce set up aviation licensing laws in 1926, Banning became the first black pilot to be licensed in America.

By 1929, when William Powell recruited Banning to become the chief pilot of the Bessie Coleman Aero Club, Banning was the most experienced black pilot in the country. He was a seasoned barnstormer with more than 750 hours of flying time to his credit. This experience qualified him not only to carry passengers but also to fly mail and other cargo.

Edna Gayle remembered William Powell's fondness for James Herman Banning:

> He wrote about Banning practically every letter he wrote. He did tell us that he and Banning wanted to be the first [black pilots] to fly from Los Angeles to Chicago nonstop. They're supposed to have started out together and went down in a desert. I don't know what desert it was. But they went down in the desert and for days they were lost.

For pilots, getting lost was quite easy in the early days. Aviators flew by what was known as "dead reckoning." They figured out their position based on air speed, how long they'd been flying, and visual landmarks on the ground. If clouds blocked their view, there were no sophisticated instruments to help the pilots find their way. Marie Coker remembered getting lost in a bad storm with Banning:

> Banning was flying the plane and I just started raising Cain. I told him I thought I saw an opening in the clouds back there.... Banning took that plane right through the clouds, through that opening, and we didn't know if we were going to hit a mountain or not. But I said a little prayer, and we came right down in the Riverside area and landed in an orange grove.

During this time, several black pilots had tried to raise money for a transcontinental flight. After all, Charles Lindbergh had crossed the Atlantic in 1927, and many white pilots had already flown across the United States.

Hubert Julian was the first black pilot to attempt to raise money for the cross-country trip. When Julian's plans to buy a sleek Lockheed airplane fell through, Banning picked up the ball and, for $450, purchased a secondhand Eagle Rock, a World War I–era plane with a 14-year-old engine. Banning then enlisted a top-notch mechanic, Thomas C. Allen, to fly with him.

Banning (right) and Allen called themselves the "Flying Hobos."

J. Herman Banning
Pilot

Thomas C. Allen,
Mec.

With their historic transcontinental flight, Banning and Allen became heroes.

Even though Banning had flown nearly 1,500 hours by this time, racial barriers prevented him from winning financial support for a cross-country trip. Long-distance flights of the 1930s were usually funded by big companies, and few businesses were willing to support black pilots. So Banning and his mechanic were left to their own resources.

But Banning made the most of this dilemma. He turned his frustrations into positive thinking. "Fine," Banning said to Allen. "We'll call ourselves the 'Flying Hobos.'"

With sheer determination and swashbuckling grit, the Flying Hobos, Banning and Allen, flew from Los Angeles on September 18, 1932. They took a southern route, "hoboing" their way across the country, relying on cleverness and good luck to keep them flying. When they landed or were forced down by bad weather, Banning and Allen would seek black sections of town where they were usually fed and housed for free.

Banning and Allen were greeted with amazement when they landed in rural airfields or on farmland. In 1932, many people's hopes and high spirits had been crushed by the unemployment and poverty of the Great Depression. For some Americans, the flight of Banning and Allen was one of the few lights in a dark period.

As they inched their way toward New York, the Flying Hobos became heroes and celebrities—even in the white press. This kind of attention was a first for black aviators. One newspaper exclaimed:

> What will come of this flight and this record remains to be seen. But it is certainly stimulating that we have heroes who come to light in this very worst of times.

Banning and Allen had started their trip with less than $100 to buy gasoline and oil. But they used their wits to raise money along the way. In Tulsa, Oklahoma, low on cash, the pair approached William Skelly, the founder of Skelly Oil Company. Skelly was an aviation buff, but he didn't like being pursued aggressively in his company offices. When his anger died down, Skelly became intrigued by Banning and Allen's story. He agreed to allow them to purchase gas and oil on credit between Tulsa and St. Louis, Missouri.

In St. Louis, engine trouble threatened to put an end to the cross-country trip. With the help of white students at a trade school, Banning and Allen took apart the Eagle Rock's engine and found the source of their trouble. The plane's engine valves needed to be replaced—but no new valves were available! The pilots panicked until an instructor pointed out that the 1928 Nash automobile used the same engine valves as the Eagle Rock. Soon, with valves from a '28 Nash, the retooled engine was purring once more.

Later, in Pittsburgh, Pennsylvania, the Flying Hobos met a man named Robert Vann at the YMCA. Vann was working with the Franklin Delano Roosevelt-John Nance Garner Democratic presidential campaign. Once Vann heard Banning and Allen's story, he came up with an idea.

*This illustration, printed in the **Chicago Defender** in 1933, shows that Banning died trying to further the advancement of blacks in aviation.*

Banning and Allen would litter the countryside between Pittsburgh and New York with 15,000 Roosevelt-Garner campaign flyers. In exchange, the Democratic Party would assist the pilots with money to fly back to California.

On Sunday morning, October 9, 1932, Banning and Allen landed at Valley Stream Airfield on Long Island, New York, three weeks after their departure from Los Angeles. Their actual time in the air had been less than 42 hours.

Banning and Allen were given the keys to New York City by Mayor Jimmy Walker. They were wined and dined by the famous musicians Duke Ellington and Cab Calloway at the Cotton Club in Harlem.

Banning and Allen returned to Los Angeles where Banning continued organizing and flying in air shows. On February 5, 1933, in San Diego, California, a biplane in which Banning was a passenger crashed to the ground while hundreds of people looked on in horror. Banning was killed. He was just 32. Great sorrow swept the nation's black communities, but Banning's adventurous spirit would long be remembered.

HUBERT FAUNTLEROY JULIAN

The Black Eagle

*H*ubert Fauntleroy Julian was born in 1897 in the town of Port of Spain on Trinidad, an island in the West Indies. There, in 1911, Hubert saw an airplane for the first time. He was very impressed not only with the plane but also with the pilot's clothing and proud manner.

The vision of the proud aviator and the wonder of flight stayed with Hubert for the remainder of his life. The experience inspired him to become a colorful character in the field of aviation.

Hubert came from a well-to-do family that wanted the best for their bright, handsome young son. Believing their son would be better educated in England than he would be in Trinidad, Hubert's parents sent him to London to attend school.

By 1914, however, World War I was gripping the European continent, and Hubert's family thought it best that he leave England. In August 1914, Julian sailed off to Canada to continue his education.

He settled in Montreal, Quebec, and lived with West Indian friends. The vision of the pilot in Port of Spain had stayed with him, and he looked for someone to take him up in an airplane. The airfield in Montreal was called St. Hubert, which Julian took as a good sign. He began to spend all his free time there.

Finally, World War I hero William "Billy" Bishop noticed this everyday visitor to the airfield. But Hubert Julian did not stick out because of his race. There were nearly 20,000 blacks living in Montreal at the time. Rather, young Hubert stood out because of his persistence, intelligence, and proud manner. On a chilly day in November 1919, Billy Bishop took an excited Hubert Fauntleroy Julian for a ten-minute ride in a Sopwith Camel.

After this memorable experience, Julian knew he wanted to learn to fly. Unlike Bessie Coleman, William Powell, and James Herman Banning though, Julian did not have trouble finding someone to teach him—especially since he had been introduced to flight by the renowned Billy Bishop.

Combat pilots like Billy Bishop inspired many black flyers.

Hubert Julian (left) and William Powell

By the time Julian moved to New York City in 1921, he was a "gentle-man flyer," sharp dresser, and man-about-town. Julian lived in Harlem for several years and became quite well known in and around New York City.

Among the noteworthy feats of the Black Eagle, as Julian was known, was his bold parachute jump from an airplane onto 139th Street in Harlem in April 1923. This feat brought considerable attention both to Julian and to blacks in aviation. The jump also earned Julian a ticket from the New York City police for causing a traffic jam.

In July 1924, Julian intended to fly to Africa and thereby become the first person to fly solo across the Atlantic Ocean. He dubbed his air-plane *Ethiopia I* and set out to raise money for the flight.

But Julian never made it farther than New York's Flushing Bay, where the *Ethiopia I* rammed into the water. Julian spent the next month in Flushing Hospital recovering from injuries. He did receive a lot of press coverage, as the *New York Sun*, the *New York Herald Tribune*, and the *New York Times* all reported on Julian's embarrassing flight.

Over the next few years, Julian crisscrossed the United States, flying and parachute jumping. In his travels, he bridged the gap between the black aviation communities in Los Angeles and Chicago. The black aero clubs in Los Angeles and Chicago were doing similar work. But they had little contact with each other, other than through Julian.

By the time Julian landed in Los Angeles to prepare for the second all-black air show in late 1931, he had made quite a name for himself in New York City and had become a media sensation.

Even though Julian was the featured performer in the air show, he disappointed the large crowd. Marie Coker remembered the reason:

> The first plane was led by William Powell. Then there was Aikens and Wells. Then Johnson and me. And Julian took up the rear. See, we made an arrow. Our instructions were to go across the Los Angeles River up to Jefferson Boulevard, where there was an airfield in case we had to land. Then we would bear to our left, turn around, and come back. And each one would land. Well, we did it. Everybody did what they were supposed to do except Colonel Julian.

"We ain't seen Julian yet," she joked years later. Several of the early black flyers resented Julian. In many ways, they felt, he embarrassed them. Julian would make grand promises—schemes to fly across the Atlantic. But when the moment of truth came, he wasn't so much interested in flying as he was in pursuing his own fame.

Julian received more press coverage than the other black flyers though, and his high profile brought him to the attention of Haile Selassie, Emperor of Ethiopia. Haile Selassie invited Julian to come to Ethiopia and organize a national air force. Julian jumped at the offer and set off for the East African nation.

Julian in Ethiopia (left) and meeting with reporters upon returning to New York (bottom)

In 1930, Haile Selassie had started a modernization program in Ethiopia. It was Julian's job to put the country on wings. But the project did not work out the way Julian planned. Early Chicago flyer Cornelius Coffey recalled: "Hubert Julian messed up in Ethiopia. If you remember, he wrecked the only [good] airplane that they had."

What's more, Italy, under dictator Benito Mussolini, claimed Ethiopia as its own territory and invaded the nation in 1935. With the Italian invasion and the loss of his best plane, Haile Selassie was unable to carry out his dream of creating a national air force. Hubert Julian returned to the United States.

He traveled to Chicago and asked the all-black Challenger Air Pilots Association to support him in another attempt to fly the Atlantic. But Julian had lost so much respect with his failed efforts, both in Ethiopia and on the West Coast, that the club turned him down.

Julian did not go away quietly, though. He continued to fly and travel throughout the world. In his later years, he became an unofficial ambassador to various nations—visiting with leaders and politicians in his typical showy fashion. The Black Eagle, the colorful Trinidadian aviator, made a lasting impression upon the history of American aviation.

Cornelius Coffey (front) and other students at the Curtiss-Wright Aeronautical School in Chicago, 1931

THE CHICAGO FLYERS

*I*n the 1920s and 1930s, Chicago was a growing metropolis—"the Hub of the Nation," a switching point for the country's railroads. There, any man, regardless of color, could find work if he were mechanically inclined. As in Los Angeles, black businesses were on the rise.

After World War I, blacks came to Chicago in great numbers, and a prominent black culture began to grow. The black community was able to support many activities, including aviation. Chicago's black aviation community, which consisted of about 30 flyers, was led by John Robinson, Willa Brown, Chauncey Spencer, Janet Waterford Bragg, Cornelius Coffey, and Harold Hurd.

Bessie Coleman inspired the Chicago flyers as much as she inspired the black aviators in Los Angeles. The Chicago flyers were the ones who made sure that every Memorial Day somebody flew over Bessie Coleman's grave and dropped a wreath of flowers.

46

This tribute to Bessie Coleman was just one small way for the Chicago aviators to recognize the contributions of their hometown hero. Like Bessie Coleman and the black pilots in Los Angeles, the Chicago flyers organized air shows and set aviation records.

Although recognition for their accomplishments was hard to come by, blacks in Chicago were able to create a legacy of flight. Chicago's Harlem Airport was a center of black aviation activity. There, master mechanic Cornelius Coffey trained many black flyers. Coffey, a certified pilot himself, took his first airplane ride in 1919. He recalled:

> There was a barnstormer at my home, and he came in giving rides. He was charging a dollar and fifty cents for a ride. So my buddy decided that he was going to dare me to take a ride in this airplane. I heard the pilot tell one of the fellows, "He'll never even look at another airplane, let alone take a ride."

The pilot performed all sorts of daring stunts, trying to scare Coffey away from flying. "Man, I almost got into a tailspin trying to excite him," the pilot said.

But instead of being frightened, Cornelius Coffey became hooked on aviation. Like Powell and Banning, Coffey was an auto mechanic who transferred his knowledge to airplanes. Coffey remembered:

> In those days, they didn't have a variety of aircraft engines. They used to convert Chevrolet and Ford engines and motorcycle engines. Of course, the real little engine that was popular at that time was a Henderson, four-cylinder motorcycle engine.

Curtiss-Wright, one of the largest airplane makers in the world at the time, operated a flight training school in Chicago. With pressure from the local black aviation community, as well as the National Association for the Advancement of Colored People (NAACP), the school

Curtiss-Wright aviation students learn to repair airplane engines.

began admitting blacks in 1930. Harold Hurd was in the first all-black class. He recalled:

> As a child I always wanted to fly. I always had that desire to get up in the air. But what [inspired] me more was Lindbergh's flight across the ocean. And I said, "That's it." My desire was to become an aeronautical engineer because I was handy at mechanical drawing and drafting. But I came along during the Depression. My family could not afford to send me to college. So . . . I said, "Well, if I can't become an engineer, I'll just learn to fly."

The Curtiss-Wright Aeronautical School trained many black flyers like Hurd. Eventually, Cornelius Coffey would start his own aviation school, the Coffey School of Aeronautics, with the help of his friend and colleague John Robinson.

Like Coffey, John Robinson loved to fly and wanted to promote aviation in the black community. Robinson and Coffey organized the all-black Challenger Air Pilots Association in 1931. Because most airports were segregated in those days, the association had to build an airstrip in a black community. After securing space in the black township of Robbins, Illinois, in 1933, the group's next big step was to find an airplane. Cornelius Coffey recalled:

> About six or seven months later, someone had an ad in the paper. They were taking an automobile as a trade on an airplane. So this used-car dealer had this airplane, and he was willing to take Johnny's car in [trade] on this Hummingbird.

Willa Brown, public relations person for the club, proved very successful at getting press coverage for Challenger air shows. Enoch Waters, city editor of the *Chicago Defender*, remembered seeing Brown for the first time:

> When Willa Brown, a young woman wearing white jodhpurs, jacket, and boots, strode into our newsroom in 1936, she made such a stunning appearance that all the typewriters, which had been clacking noisily, suddenly went silent. . . . She had a confident bearing and there was an undercurrent of determination in her voice. . . . In a businesslike manner she explained that she was an aviatrix and wanted some publicity for a Negro air show at Harlem Airport on the city's southwest side. . . . Fascinated both by her and the idea of Negro aviators, I decided to follow up the story myself. . . . So happy was Willa over our appearance that she offered to take me up for a free ride. She was piloting a Piper Cub. . . . It was a thrilling experience, and the maneuvers—figure eights, flipovers and stalls—were exhilarating, though momentarily frightening. I wasn't convinced of her competence until we landed smoothly.

In addition to operating the Challenger Air Pilots Association,

Robinson, Coffey, Brown, and the other Chicago flyers tried to interest Tuskegee Institute in building an aviation program. Coffey recalled:

> We flew to Tuskegee with the idea of trying to encourage them to include aviation in their program. But at the time, they weren't interested in aviation. So that kind of disappointed us, because on that trip, by the way, we came very near to losing our life. In fact, we lost an airplane.

As the Chicago aero club grew, the aviators became frustrated that neither Tuskegee nor the U.S. military would train blacks as combat pilots. The Chicago flyers had heard about efforts to organize an Ethiopian air force, and Cornelius Coffey, John Robinson, and Willa Brown all longed to assist Haile Selassie and Hubert Julian in Ethiopia. John Robinson did join Julian in Africa for a short time, but he returned to Chicago after the Italian invasion of Ethiopia in 1935.

Coffey, Hurd, Robinson, and others in Chicago next turned their attention to the United States government. The pilots hoped to convince government officials to accept blacks in the Civilian Pilot Training Program (CPT), a flight school established by Congress to prepare civilian pilots for wartime emergency.

This time, the Chicago flyers were successful. With the assistance of the NAACP and other groups, the Chicago flyers persuaded the government to open up the CPT to blacks in 1939. For the first time, black pilots had access to U.S. government flight training.

The role of blacks in aviation was changing. Blacks had shown they indeed had the ability to fly, and black pilots were finally being recognized as important participants in the growing field of aviation. Tuskegee Institute would soon become the central training ground for black combat pilots. Many CPT graduates would go on to become Tuskegee Airmen.

Female aviators Janet Waterford Bragg (top) and Willa Brown (left) carried on in Chicago after Bessie Coleman's death.

The Tuskegee Airmen of World War II

Black navigators at Hondo Field, Texas, 1945

The idea of a government-supported black air force started in the 1930s with Haile Selassie's efforts in Ethiopia. In the United States, though, the military was still segregated and racially discriminatory. Black soldiers were barred from aviation training.

With the U.S. entry into World War II in 1941, aviation took on added importance in the United States. The U.S. Army Air Corps, the Army's aviation division, needed fighter pilots. With some reluctance, the Army agreed to allow black soldiers to train for aviation combat at Tuskegee Army Airfield in Alabama. This training program, which took place between 1941 and 1945, became known as the "Tuskegee Experiment."

When the all-black 99th Fighter Squadron was sent into action in March 1941, blacks had finally become part of military aviation in the United States. But the Army was still segregated. The black pilots who trained at the Tuskegee Army Airfield essentially belonged to a separate black air force.

In the war over Europe, the 99th Fighter Squadron joined the 100th, the 301st, and the 302nd, to form the all-black 332nd Fighter Group. The black fighter squadrons flew in Allied campaigns in North Africa, Sicily, Italy, and Germany. They escorted bombers, fired on enemy positions in support of Allied ground forces, and engaged in air combat. Called the "Red Tails" because of the distinctive tail markings on their aircraft, the 332nd fighter pilots became known for their effectiveness.

The Tuskegee Experiment had been a success. Just as the Bessie Coleman Aero Club and the Challenger Air Pilots Association proved that blacks were capable civilian pilots, the Tuskegee Experiment proved that blacks could be trained in large numbers for combat flying. The

The first class of Tuskegee cadets, 1941

Lieutenant Colonel Benjamin O. Davis, commander of the World War II black fighter squadrons

abilities of the black pilots and the skillful leadership of their commander, Lieutenant Colonel Benjamin O. Davis, Jr., helped ease white hostility toward blacks in military aviation.

But bias and discrimination still dogged the black fighter pilots—just as it had the pioneer black aviators. While the black flyers in World War II fought for democracy overseas, they faced denial of their civil rights at home.

The success of the black combat pilots helped spark a renewed sense of pride among black Americans, though. The achievements of the black flyers not only expanded the opportunities for blacks in aviation but also brought more urgency to the call for desegregation of the U.S. armed forces.

In 1948, President Harry S. Truman signed Executive Order 9981—calling for desegregation of the United States military—into law. Order 9981 was the first legal call for desegregation in the country. In 1949, the newly established United States Air Force became the first armed service to put the law into place. The integration of the armed forces was a crucial event. It had a ripple effect that led to the integration of much of American society.

Perhaps the early black aviation pioneers, like William J. Powell, James Herman Banning, Bessie Coleman, and others, were correct in thinking that equality in the air would bring equality on the ground as well.

President Truman meets with some of the military and political leaders who drafted Executive Order 9981.

MODERN AVIATION AND BLACK FLYERS

Helicopter pilot Perry H. Young, Jr.

*H*aving proven their abilities during World War II, black military pilots also flew during the Korean War and the Vietnam War. The civil rights era of the 1960s helped blacks move into commercial aviation. Many black flyers have made careers in the airline industry.

Encouraged by Cornelius Coffey and Willa Brown, Perry H. Young, Jr., learned to fly in the 1930s. He worked as a flight instructor both at the Coffey School of Aeronautics in Chicago and at Tuskegee Army Airfield during World War II. In 1956, Young was hired as a helicopter pilot by New York Airways.

James O. Plinton, Jr., was also a flight instructor at Tuskegee Army Airfield. He became an airline executive and held positions at both Trans World Airlines and Eastern Airlines. David E. Harris joined American Airlines in the mid-1960s, thus becoming one of the first black pilots to be employed by a major airline.

In 1965, after a long court battle, Marlon D. Green became a commercial pilot with Continental Airlines (the airline had tried to deny Green his position). His successful legal battle opened the doors wider for black pilots in the airline industry.

Some black pilots have moved into the U.S. space program. Dr. Vance H. Marchbanks, Jr., an Air Force flight surgeon and former member of the 332nd Fighter Group, worked with the National Aeronautics and Space Administration (NASA) in the 1960s. When John Glenn, the first American to orbit the Earth, went into space in February 1962, Marchbanks served on Glenn's mission control team.

Captain Edward J. Dwight, Jr., the first black astronaut candidate, was nominated for space flight training in 1963. Dwight was passed over when the astronaut selections were made, however, and charges of racial discrimination were raised with his dismissal.

The first black astronaut in space was Colonel Guion S. Bluford, Jr. Bluford, an Air Force pilot who flew 144 combat missions in Vietnam, was a mission specialist on NASA's *Challenger* space shuttle flight in 1983. Another black astronaut, Ronald E. McNair, lost his life when the *Challenger* space shuttle exploded in 1986. This tragedy reminds us that flight remains a dangerous undertaking, as the pioneer black flyers knew well.

Despite progress in commercial aviation and space flight, there are still too few black pilots. Out of approximately 54,000 commercial pilots in the United States, only about 400 are black. Sixty years ago, William J. Powell called for "black wings to take to the sky." His words still ring true.

The early black aviators made a significant contribution to American history. Their important story, overlooked until recent times, is one of people overcoming barriers to succeed in a field of technology.

The early black aviators set the stage for the success of the Tuskegee Airmen and the modern black flyers. During the golden age of aviation, the dream for all pioneer aviators was to create another generation of pilots. As Harold Hurd said in 1985:

Guion Bluford

We have always prayed and we have always hoped, some-
day in the future there would be guys like Guy Bluford,
and then our work would not have been in vain.

When Colonel Guion Bluford, America's first black astronaut in space,
met Cornelius Coffey, one of America's oldest black aviators, it was
clear that each man thought of the other as an inspiration and a hero.
Cornelius Coffey recalled:

Bluford said to me that he was wondering if he would ever
get the chance to meet me. And I said, "Well I wondered the
same about you."

Progress is made by those who dare—those who stand up and take risks. The early black aviators risked their lives and what little money they had, and often they faced only ridicule as their reward. But it is through the lives of these early pioneers that the dream of flight lives on.

Harold Hurd

Resources and Further Reading

Flyers in Search of a Dream. Philip Hart, UCLA and WGBH-Boston, 1987. Distributed by PBS Video, Public Broadcasting Service, 1988.

———————

At the Controls: Women in Aviation. Carole S. Briggs. Minneapolis: Lerner Publications Company, 1991.

Black Wings: The American Black in Aviation. Von Hardesty and Dominick Pisano. Washington: National Air and Space Museum, Smithsonian Institution Press, 1984.

Space Challenger: The Story of Guion Bluford. Jim Haskins and Kathleen Benson. Minneapolis: Carolrhoda Books, 1983.

The Tuskegee Airmen. Charles E. Francis. Boston: Branden Publishing Company, 1988.

*A. Porter Davis, Willa Brown, and Cornelius Coffey at Harlem Airport,
August 1939*

INDEX

Cornelius Coffey (left) greets Dale L. White and Chauncey E. Spencer after their 3,000-mile round-trip flight from Chicago to Washington D.C.

ACKNOWLEDGMENTS

Photographs and illustrations reproduced with permission of Smithsonian Institution, pp. 2, 11 (left and right), 14, 16 (top and bottom), 21, 46, 51 (left and right), 59, 61, 64; Philip S. Hart, pp. 8, 12, 26, 28, 29, 33, 35, 38, 40, 42, 44 (top and bottom), 48, 54; North Carolina Department of Commerce, p. 9; Northrop University, pp. 13, 22, 25; Philips Petroleum Company, p. 19; Imperial War Museum, London, p. 30; Thomas C. Allen, p. 36; Public Archives Canada, Ottawa, p. 41; Schomburg Center for Research in Black Culture, p. 52; United States Air Force, pp. 53, 55; Perry H. Young, Jr., p. 56; National Aeronautics and Space Administration, p. 58.

Cover photographs courtesy of Smithsonian Institution (top and bottom right), Philip S. Hart (bottom left and back cover).

DATE DUE

DEMCO 38-297

About the Book

GEORGE W. ALLEN was proud of two things. His name and his birthday. He was named for George Washington and he had the same birthday. It made him feel almost related. So related he wanted to know everything he could about George Washington.

George wanted to know the *important* things — he already knew the names of Washington's dogs and what size shoes he wore, but he didn't know what George Washington ate for breakfast. He got his grandmother to promise she'd cook George Washington's breakfast if he found out what it was, and he was going to find out — no matter what.

The whole family and even the town librarian joined George in his search, which included exploring sources from the card catalogue to a trip to Mount Vernon. Told with humor and a keen sense of factual detail, this story brings history to life with a freshness and excitement that will delight every child. Paul Galdone's colorful illustrations are rich in historical accuracy as well as lively imagination.

George Washington's Breakfast

by Jean Fritz

Paul Galdone drew the pictures

COWARD-McCANN, INC.   NEW YORK

For
Carol Louise Kelly

Grateful acknowledgment is made to the Mattatuck Historical Association of Waterbury, Connecticut, and to Mr. Rawson W. Haddon for the title and the idea of this book, taken from *George Washington's Breakfast*, Occasional Publications, No. 26.

Library of Congress Catalog Card Number: 69-11475
ISBN 0-698-30099-8 (hc)
11   13   15   17   19   20   18   16   14   12
First paperback edition, 1984.
ISBN 0-698-20616-9 (pbk)
9   10

George Washington's Breakfast

G eorge W. Allen was proud of two things.
His name and his birthday.

George was named for George Washington. And he had the same birthday. February 22.

It made him feel almost related, he said.

It made him want to know everything there was to know about George Washington.

Already he knew quite a lot. He knew that Washington was a general and lived in Virginia and was six feet tall and married to Martha and was the first President of the United States.

He knew that Washington rode two horses in the war, Blueskin and Nelson, but Nelson was his favorite because he was so steady in gunfire.

He also knew that Washington once had ten hunting dogs. Their names were: Tipsey, Pompey, Harry, Maiden, Lady, Dutchess, Drunkard, Tru-Love, Mopsy, and Pilot.

Then one day at breakfast George Allen thought of something he didn't know. George's mother and father had gone
to work, and his grandmother was frying eggs at the kitchen
stove.

"Grandma," George said, "what did George Washington
eat for breakfast?"

"Search me," his grandmother said. "That was before my time." She put a plate of fried eggs in front of George. "And don't you expect me to help you find out either."

George's grandmother knew what George was like. When George wanted to find out something, he didn't rest until he found out. He didn't let anyone else rest either. He did just what his grandfather used to do — ask questions, collect books, and pester everyone for answers. And George's grandmother wasn't going to fool around now about breakfasts that were over and done with two hundred years ago. Besides, there was the spring housecleaning to do.

George punctured the two fried eggs on his plate. "Well," he said, "if I find out, will you do one thing for me?"

"What's that?"

"Will you cook me George Washington's breakfast?"

George's grandmother looked at the clock on the kitchen wall. "George," she said, "you'll be late for school."

"But will you?" George insisted. "Will you cook me George Washington's breakfast?"

George's grandmother was still looking at the clock. "I'll cook anything," she said, "as long as you hurry."

After school that day George Allen went to the library. Miss Willing, the librarian, smiled when she saw him come in the door. "I wonder what that Allen boy wants to know now," she thought.

George walked up to the desk. "Miss Willing," he said, "do you know what George Washington ate for breakfast?"

Miss Willing could hardly remember what *she'd* had for breakfast that morning, but like George, she liked to find out answers.

Together George and Miss Willing went to the encyclopedia and looked under *W.* "Washington, George." The encyclopedia said Washington was born in 1732, married in 1759, elected President in 1789 and died in 1799. It told all about the years when he took trips and fought battles and did other important things. But it didn't say what he did everyday. It didn't mention his breakfasts.

Miss Willing took George to the card catalogue where every book in the whole library was written down on a separate card with a number or letter that told where you could find it. George liked opening the little drawers of the catalogue and finding the right drawer and flipping through the cards until he found what he wanted. There were seven books about George Washington. Most of them were in the section of the library marked *B* for Biography.

George picked out four books to take home, and Miss Willing promised that she would look at the rest.

That night after supper George gave his father a book to read, and he gave his mother a book to read.

"Don't look at me," his grandmother said. "I said I'd cook but I wouldn't look."

So George kept the other two books for himself. All evening George and his mother and father read.

George was very excited when he found out that Washington liked to count things. George liked to count things too. George had counted how many steps there were between his house and the school. And there was Washington back in the 1700's counting steps too! It made George feel more related than ever.

The book said that once Washington figured out that there were 71,000 seeds in a pound of red clover. And 844,800 seeds in a pound of Red River grass.

But there wasn't a word about Washington's breakfasts, and the way George figured it, Washington must have eaten breakfast more than 24,000 times.

Then all at once Mrs. Allen looked up. "Listen to this," she said. "This book says that in Washington's time breakfast in Virginia usually consisted of cold turkey, cold meat, fried hominy, toast, cider, ham, bread and butter, tea, coffee and chocolate."

Then all at once Mrs. Allen looked up. "Listen to this," she said. "This book says that in Washington's time breakfast in Virginia usually consisted of cold turkey, cold meat, fried hominy, toast, cider, ham, bread and butter, tea, coffee and chocolate."

George Allen felt his mouth beginning to water. He grinned and looked at his grandmother.

"Humph!" his grandmother scoffed. "Notice the book said what was *usual* in Virginia. Everyone knows George Washington was an unusual man. No telling what he ate."

A little later Mr. Allen looked up from his book. "Guess what?" he said. "It says here that people in Washington's day didn't eat a real breakfast. Instead they had lunch at ten o'clock in the morning."

George Allen's grandmother grinned and looked at George.

"Doesn't mean a thing," George said. "That book's talking about Washington's day. Not about George Washington."

The day the Allens finished reading their four books was a Saturday, a nice, sunny spring Saturday. George Allen's grandmother took down the curtains to wash. His mother hung the winter clothes outside.

George went back to the library. Miss Willing suggested that they find out what some of George Washington's friends had to say.

First they read from the diary of John Adams, who was the second President of the United States. John Adams wrote that George Washington ruined his teeth when he was a boy by cracking walnuts in his mouth.

Thomas Jefferson, the third President of the United States, wrote that Washington was the best horseman of his age.

General Lafayette, who helped Washington fight the Revolutionary War, wrote that George Washington wore a size

13 shoe and had the biggest hands he'd ever seen. It was said that he could bend a horseshoe with his bare hands.

No one mentioned if George Washington ever ate or not.

Day after day George and his mother and father and Miss Willing read. George's grandmother started to clean the attic.

Then one day Miss Willing said the reading was over. There were no more books in the library about George Washington. Of course there were bigger libraries, she pointed out. George could go to one of them.

But George had a different idea. "We'll go to Washington's home in Mount Vernon, Virginia," he said, "where George Washington's breakfasts were actually cooked."

The next weekend George and Mr. and Mrs. Allen got in the car. They asked George's grandmother to come, but she said, no, she'd cook, but she wouldn't look. Besides, she was glad to get rid of them, she said. She'd have the attic to herself. No one could poke around trying to rescue things that should be thrown out.

On the way to Mount Vernon, George and his mother and father stopped at Washington, D.C. George wanted to go to the Smithsonian Institution, a museum that had all kinds of historical exhibits — log cabins, covered wagons, and glass cases full of old guns and old coins and old knives and old watches.

"You won't find George Washington's breakfast here," Mr. Allen said. "He ate his breakfasts. He didn't put them in a glass case."

George said that in such a big museum a person couldn't tell what he'd find.

He didn't expect to see George Washington himself, and he certainly didn't expect to see him dressed in a curtain. George's father said that Washington was wearing a Roman toga. Not that he had ever worn a Roman toga, but the sculptor thought he'd look nice in it. George wondered if Washington was embarrassed by the toga, but he decided he wasn't. Washington looked calm and rather satisfied, George thought. As a matter of fact, Washington looked as if he'd just eaten a nice breakfast. But there was no way to tell what the breakfast was. There was nothing in the museum that told about Washington's breakfast.

Still, George did see the uniform that Washington wore on December 23, 1783, when he resigned from the Army. It was a black and tan uniform, and it had white ruffles and brass buttons. Every place George looked there were brass buttons — down the front of the jacket, on the vest, at the back of the neck, on the sleeves and pockets, on the tails of the coat and at the knees. George walked all around the uniform and counted the buttons. There were 64 brass buttons.

Then George walked back to the statue. "I bet you and I," he said, "are the only ones in the world who ever counted up all those buttons."

At Mount Vernon George and his mother and father went right to the kitchen. They walked on the same path that Washington had walked on, and every time George put his feet down, he thought of Washington's size 13's in the same spot.

The kitchen was in a separate building at the side of the house. It was a large room with a big brick fireplace at one end and brass pots and iron pots and griddles and pans and ladles hanging on the walls. George held his breath. It was at that very fireplace, he told himself, that Washington's breakfasts had been cooked. The food may actually have been in some of those very pots and pans. Suddenly George felt so related to Washington that goose pimples broke out on his arm.

He turned to a guard in uniform standing at the door. "Can you tell me," George said, "what George Washington ate for breakfast?"

The guard spoke as if he were reciting a lesson. "Breakfast was at seven. The guests were served tea and coffee and meat, both cold and boiled."

"And did Washington eat the same breakfast?"

The guard looked confused. "I don't know," he said. "I've only been here eight months."

This wasn't enough for George. Yet it seemed to him that the answer must be in the room itself. Maybe if he closed his eyes, the answer would come.

So George closed his eyes. He waited, and he listened. After a while he thought he heard a little crackling noise at the far end of the room. He guessed it might be the fire coming back in the fireplace. Then outside he heard a dog bark. Pompey, he thought. Or maybe Drunkard.

George squeezed his eyes even tighter and he listened even harder. Then he felt a shadow at the door. There was a very thin, ghosty-sounding whisper; George had to strain to hear it.

"I served the guests," the voice said. "Now you got the general's breakfast ready?"

George was so excited he snapped his eyes open. But there was no fire in the fireplace. There was no one talking; there were no signs of breakfast. He supposed he'd opened his eyes too soon, but when he tried to go back, it was no use. It was all gone. And the guard was giving him a funny look.

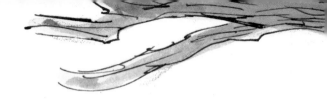

On Sunday afternoon George and his father and mother went home. They found George's grandmother and Miss Willing waiting together on the front porch.

"No luck," George reported. He was sorry that everyone was so disappointed, but he thought they should be planning what to do next.

Instead, Mr. Allen put his hand on George's shoulder. "It was a good try, son," he said. "You can't win them all."

"Sometimes there's nothing to do but give up," Mrs. Allen said.

George's grandmother said she guessed in the long run it didn't matter so much what George Washington ate.

George Allen looked at his family in amazement. "*Give up!*" he shouted. "You expect me to give up! George Washington's soldiers were starving, and they didn't give up. They were freezing, and they didn't give up. *What do you think I am?*"

George was so mad he slammed the screen door and went up to his room. But even upstairs he could hear them talking to Miss Willing about him. George stamped up to the attic. He sat down on the top step. It was quiet here. And very neat. He could see his grandmother had been working.

Next to him was a box filled with things he guessed his grandmother meant to throw away. On top of the box was an old stuffed dog. He remembered that dog. His name was Ginger. One ear was torn now, and the tail was hanging by a thread. Still, he was a good dog. George put him aside.

He looked back in the box. There was a bunch of old Batman comics. It was a good thing he'd come up here, he thought. No one should throw away old comics.

Under the comics George found a book. It was an old book, torn and beat-up-looking — probably his grandfather's, he thought, and it seemed a shame to throw it away. *The American Oracle*, the book was called, and it was written by the Honorable Samuel Stearns, whoever that was.

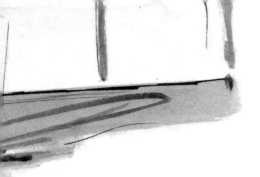

George whistled as he turned the pages. This honorable Samuel Stearns thought he knew *everything*. He told you how to choose a wife, how to kill bedbugs and how to keep from getting bald. He named the birds of North America (140), and he listed all the famous earthquakes since the year 17 (63 earthquakes). Then there was a chapter called "The Character of Washington."

George looked back at the title page where he knew he would find the date that the book was published.

"1791," he read. Samuel Stearns was living at the same time as Washington.

George turned back to the chapter on Washington. "Well, Mr. Stearns," George said, "if you know so much, kindly inform me about Washington's breakfast."

"Washington," Mr. Stearns wrote, "raised 7,000 bushels of wheat and 10,000 bushels of corn in one year."

"Okay, okay," George said. "That wasn't the question."

"Washington," Mr. Stearns continued, "is very regular, temperate, and industrious; rises winter and summer at dawn of day."

"Then what?" George asked.

"He breakfasts about seven," Mr. Stearns wrote, "on —"

Suddenly George let out a whoop. He put the book behind his back and clattered down the steps.

"Grandma!" he shouted. "When did you say you'd cook me George Washington's breakfast?"

"Boy, if you ever find out about that breakfast, I'll cook it right then no matter what time it is."

"Right this minute, for instance?"

"That's what I said."

George grinned. "Grandma," he said, "put on your apron." He brought the book out from behind his back.

"Washington," he read, "breakfasts about seven o'clock on three small Indian hoecakes and as many dishes of tea."

George passed the book around, and he thought he'd never seen people act as happy. All but his grandmother.

"George," she said, "I don't have the slightest idea what an Indian hoecake is."

George went to the dictionary. He looked under *H*. "Hoe-cake. A cake of cornmeal and water and salt baked before an open fire or in the ashes, originally on a hoe."

George's grandmother put on her apron. "I've cornmeal and water and salt," she said. "I guess I can make some Indian hoecakes."

George's father built a fire in the fireplace.

George's mother filled the kettle with water for the tea.

George said he'd go down to the basement for a hoe, but his grandmother stopped him. "You don't want me to cook these things on a *hoe*, do you?" she asked.

"That's what the dictionary says."

"The dictionary says *originally*. That means when hoecakes first came out. I expect they'd been around quite a while before Washington's time."

George wasn't sure. He wanted to do it right.

"Did you see a hoe in Washington's kitchen?"

George admitted there was no hoe there.

"All right then," his grandmother said. "Did you see any black iron griddles?"

George said that he had.

"That's what we'll use," his grandmother said. She mixed cornmeal and water in a bowl; she added salt; then she shaped the mixture in her hands to form little cakes.

Everyone sat around the fire to wait for breakfast. Pretty soon the tea kettle began to steam and the hoecakes began to turn a nice golden brown.

Then George's grandmother served George Washington's breakfast.

George took a bite of hoecake. It was pretty good, he thought. He looked at his mother and his father and his grandmother and Miss Willing all eating hoecakes together on a Sunday afternoon. George decided he felt more related to Washington than he'd ever felt in his whole life. It was as if George Washington were right there at the fireplace with them. And Drunkard at his feet.

There was only one trouble.

When George finished his three small hoecakes and his three cups of tea, he was still hungry. And if he was hungry, he thought, what about Washington? For a man who was six feet tall and the Father of His Country, it seemed like a skimpy breakfast.

"I hope Washington didn't have long to wait until lunch," he said. "I hope he had a nice big lunch to look forward to. A nice big one. I wonder what —"

But George never finished his sentence. His grandmother was standing up.

"George Washington Allen," she cried. "Don't you *dare*!" And she pointed her spatula at him.

"Not today," Miss Willing said. "The library is closed today."

"Okay." George grinned. "Not today."

About the Author

JEAN FRITZ is the distinguished author of books for young people, most of which deal with American history. They include several novels and biographies of Paul Revere, Sam Adams, Patrick Henry, John Hancock, Ben Franklin and George III, as well as Stonewall Jackson, Benedict Arnold and Pocahontas. In 1982 her book *Homesick: My Own Story* won the American Book Award and was a Newbery Honor Book. Ms. Fritz and her husband live in Dobbs Ferry, New York.

About the Artist

PAUL GALDONE has retold and illustrated close to twenty classic tales, as well as illustrating another ten books, two of which were written by his daughter Joanna. He was born in Hungary and came to the United States at the age of fourteen. He studied at the Art Students League in New York City. Mr. Galdone and his wife divide their time between their Vermont farm and a home in Rockland County, New York.